A Treasury of Polish Aphorisms

A Treasury of Polish Aphorisms

COMPILED AND TRANSLATED BY JACEK GAŁĄZKA

INTRODUCTION BY JERZY R. KRZYŻANOWSKI

ILLUSTRATED BY BARBARA ŚWIDZIŃSKA

POLISH HERITAGE PUBLICATIONS

Published by Polish Heritage Publications

75 Warren Hill Road

Cornwall Bridge, CT 06754

Distributed to the book trade by

Hippocrene Books

171 Madison Avenue

New York, NY 10016

ISBN 0-7818-0549-X

Illustrations by Barbara Świdzińska

Cover and book design by Marek Antoniak

Printed in the United States of America

This book is dedicated to

Stanisław Jerzy Lec (1901-1966), a poet and

aphorist whose *Unkempt Thoughts* enriched our world.

A Treasury of Polish Aphorisms

In the early 1980s The Indiana University Polish Studies Center organized an international conference "The Polish Renaissance in its European Context" commemorating, among other things, two important anniversaries of Poland's most important poet of that period, Jan Kochanowski: the 450 years from his birthday in 1530, and 400 years since his death in 1584. An impressive volume of the conference papers, meticulously edited by Prof. Samuel Fiszman and with a foreword by Czesław Miłosz, who took an active part in the academic proceedings, appeared in 1988 under the same title, gathering under one cover twenty seven papers, ranging from historical and comparative studies to some minute, analytical discussions of Kochanowski's life and works. When asked to present a contribution I decided to focus on one of the smallest forms of his literary output, and selected one of Kochanowski's trifles, *On Human Life* (*O żywocie ludzkim*), as an example of his literary mastery which enabled him to start from the premises of seemingly minor importance, a puppet show, eventually making it into a symbol of the human condition and man's destiny. For I have always firmly believed that such a compact, terse form of a literary expression can render the major truth in quite a few cases better and more to the point than many voluminous philosophical treatises.

It was not a coincidence that Kochanowski's literary mastery dominated the 16th century Polish Renaissance. Well educated in classical studies, bilingual in Polish and Latin, the poet followed the Greek and Roman literary tradition as easily as his contemporaries in Western Europe, who not only emulated it but improved on it with their own original contributions to the genre of the precise, pointed form of the shortest and yet philosophically and literally most voluminous message, known under various names—apophthegmats, trifles or aphorisms. The great Dutch master, Erasmus of Rotterdam, as the authot of numerous works in that genre, often called apophthegmata and modeled on the works of Plato and Aristotle, was among the first ones to ponder on its very nature, and said that in its brevity it has to contain "a hidden kernel" of the great truth under an often jocular surface. His Polish contemporaries, Mikołaj Rej and Jan Kochanowski among others, followed that rule with an amazing accuracy.

As an interesting example of that genre's rising popularity we may recall an aphorism by Mikołaj Rej, dubbed "the father of Polish letters" since he broke the centuries long domination of Latin in Polish writings, and created first literary works in his native language. His famous statement, known to every school child in Poland that "the Poles have the language not of the geese but their own" (Polacy nie gęsi lecz swój język mają), has become a landmark in Polish literary history, having begun an epoch of new writing which eventually led to the mastery of Rej's contemporary, Jan Kochanowski. He elaborated his art onto a higher, philosophical level: "The laws are like spiderwebs: the sparrow flies through, the fly gets the penalty" (Prawa są równe jako pajęczyna: wróbl się przewinie, a na muszkę wina). Wit, an elegant poetic form, some scepticism and a necessary detachment provided a distance from which the author could judge his own time and mores in their forever changing shapes. And the same standard applied to the followers of that period—providing for circumstances that shaped the national destinies. Thus the century of destructive wars in the mid-1600s contributed little to literary achievements and yet introduced some baroque concepts of a sophisticated style, such as Elżbieta Drużbacka's, Wespazjan Kochowski's, or Szymon Szymonowic's aphorisms, reflecting on changing moral and social attitudes ("More courageous is he who fears not the whip but fame").

With the declining state of the country under the Saxon dynasty in the 18th century literature was on the decline too, and only in its last decades just before the partitions of Poland, it brought about the new concept of the Age of Reason represented by some of the brightest talents in arts and literature, writers such as Ignacy Krasicki, a true master of witty aphorisms. His was that famous line in a mock-heroic poem *Myszeis* (1775): My rządzimy światem, a nami kobiety (We rule the world and are being ruled by women) which, incidentally, he borrowed from the ancient author, Plutarch, but gave it a new, contemporary meaning.

It might come as a surprise to learn that such an aphorism had been made by His Excellency Bishop of Warmia but then Krasicki was not an ordinary clergyman either. One of the leading personalities of his time, a liberal and a poet with a fiercely independent mind, he often indulged in his poems and moral fables exposing human weaknesses and follies; here however the "hidden kernel" happened to be also political in nature. For *Myszeis* appeared in print three years after the first partition of Poland, accomplished by a sinister plot of two females, two powerful rulers of the neighboring countries, Catherine II of Russia, and Maria Theresa of Austria. As the Poles, at that time still in love with Latin, would say: Sapienti sat (Good enough for those who know).

The political partitions of the 1790s, which erased Poland from the map of Europe for the next 125 years, resulted not only in bloody uprisings against the Russian oppression but coincided with Poland's most glorious literary period, the Romanticism. Three majot poets of that trend, Adam Mickiewicz, Juliusz Słowacki, and Zygmunt Krasinski, followed a different creative path and yet coined some memorable poetic aphorisms (often in the form of elegant couplets), in many cases reflecting on their despair and misery as political exiles from the country partitioned by its neighbors. Only in the second half of the 19th century, when in Poland masterpieces of modern novel, short story and essays marked the new era in Polish literary history, their authors, writers such as Bolesław Prus or Henryk Sienkiewicz revived that genre with their own, philosophical aphorisms, often starting from the premises of commenting on the state of the art, literary profession, etc., and arriving at some general, universal conclusions, thus once more making the genre of aphorism a living part of modern literature.

No less prolific were the writers at the turn of the century, poets and playwrights, who often expressed their deep concern with major moral and social issues once more in the aphoristic form, while politicians, such as Józef Piłsudski, a man with love and understanding of literature, did not refrain from using it in their public addresses. Some of them, to be sure, departed from programatic themes, and simply coined some pithy aphorisms such as the one by Ignacy Paderewski, a skilled politician and a world-renowned piano virtuoso.

13

In our own 20th century, with its shattering experiences of the two World Wars with a short, twenty years long period of freedom between them, but followed by the Communist domination over Poland, the intellectual and political resistance and opposition to the idea of "captive minds" (as Czesław Miłosz phrased it), all those factors helped to refine and to sharpen the aphoristic form, often used to evade the all-controlling censorship in the years following World War II in Poland, as exemplified in the superb aphorisms of Stanisław Jerzy Lec. Suffice it to compare the carefree, funny aphorisms by Julian Tuwim, written between the wars, with Lec's biting and often bitter preoccupation with the idea of freedom, to see how the country's history reflected on such, it seemed, noncommittal form of literary expression.

Those examples should suffice to create an idea how the Polish aphorism started to develop as a literary genre, a genre different from its sister forms—folksy proverbs and moral maxims or "winged words" (as the Russians call them), the French bon mots, etc. The Polish aphorisms, from their earliest beginnings in the 16th century, up to their most contemporary examples in our own time and age have distinguished themselves by their philosophical universal contents which—unlike the mostly anonymous, folkloristic proverbs—can be applied to the state of mind rather than a given realistic situation, and contain a generally recognized truth encapsulated in the shortest possible form. And, at the same time, they often contain a message that can be easily deciphered by those who can read "between the lines," the readers sympathetic to the general idea of freedom, and opposed to any control over human minds. Thus one can easily accept a definition proposed by a Polish literary scholar, Julian Krzyżanowski, who referred to an aphorism as "a whole literary work contained in a framework of one sentence." When we examine the Polish aphorisms, from Rej and Kochanowski to Stanisław Jerzy Lec and Wojciech Młynarski, we shall not only see how appropriately that definition fits but—most of all—how the Polish aphorisms convey the basic truths in the simplest yet most sophisticated literary form. The basic truths, one can add, that are valid not only for that nation but for the human race at large, thus providing an important contribution to the understanding of our time.

—Jerzy R. Krzyżanowski, *The Ohio State University*

Polish Aphorisms

In his introduction to the first edition of Stanisław Jerzy Lec's *Unkempt Thoughts* Clifton Fadiman, American essayist and editor, wrote: "an aphorism (this one of course excepted) can contain only as much wisdom as overstatement can permit. It sells the part for the whole. Its plausibility derives from its concision, which stuns, and its wit, which dazzles. Hence our pleasure in it depends upon the partial arrest of our reasoning faculty. (This is true also of its homely cousin—the proverb, the adage and the maxim; and of its flashy younger brothers— the epigram and the paradox)". Calling Lec "a contemporary genius of the aphorism" Fadiman goes on to say: "this man is one of the notable wits of our dark time, eminently attuned to it, an unhappy man—but not to the point where he has lost the spirit to put his unhappiness into tiny perfect forms, aphorisms for an age of anxiety."

This volume of Polish aphorisms, including many of his own, is dedicated to Stanisław Jerzy Lec, a great man as well as a great aphorist and poet, whose turbulent life came to an end at the age of 56.

In selecting these aphorisms I sought to include only those that do not depend on some Polish subtext or play of words that does not translate well into English. The aphorisms included here are mostly benign, not the subtle weapons that Poles have used for many years in their struggle against tyranny. "The window to the world can be covered by a newspaper" is one such, for it did not refer to the insulating power of paper well known to those without heat and to the homeless. Lec had many fights with the communist censors over such aphorisms but today, we sincerely hope, the age of oppression in Poland is irreversibly over. Only a few of "dangerous" sayings will appear in this book, reminders of the past when many aphorisms were "on active service."

STANISŁAW JERZY LEC (1909-1966)

Z kim śpi, tego sny ma.

Sleeping with him, she dreams his dreams.

Ach, znać prywatny adres Pana Boga.

Stosy nie rozświetlają ciemności.

Legendy burzą często żądni jej surowca.

Przysłowia sobie przeczą.
I to jest właśnie mądrością ludową.

Koniom i zakochanym inaczej pachnie siano.

Nie pytaj Boga o drogę do nieba,
bo wskaże ci najtrudniejszą.

Na szyi żyrafy pchła zaczyna wierzyć
w nieśmiertelność.

22

Oh, to know God's private address.

Burning stakes do not lighten the darkness.

Legends are often destroyed by those in need of its stuff.

Proverbs contradict each other.
That is the wisdom of a people.

Hay smells different to lovers and horses.

Do not ask God for the way to heaven;
He will show you the hardest one.

On the neck of a giraffe a flea begins
to believe in immortality.

Nawet flądra nie jest bezstronna.

Pierwszym warunkiem nieśmiertelności jest śmierć.

Nie opowiadajcie swoich snów.
A może przyjdą do władzy freudyści?

"Z eunuchami można mówić długo"—opowiadała
pewna pani z haremu.

I bezstronni nie są bezstronni.
Są za sprawiedliwością.

Czy wyobrażacie sobie kobietę, która dałaby
swojemu ulubieńcowi opowiadać przez
1001 nocy bajki?

Even a flounder takes sides.

The first condition of immortality is death.

Don't tell your dreams. What if the
Freudians come to power?

"With a eunuch one can have such a nice chat,"
said the lady from a harem.

Impartiality is not neutrality.
It is partiality for justice.

Can you imagine the woman who
would let her lover tell her tales
for 1001 nights?

STANISŁAW JERZY LEC (1909-1966)

Niejeden bumerang nie wraca.
Wybiera wolność.

Not every boomerang returns.
Some choose freedom.

Przywarli do siebie tak blisko,
że nie było już miejsca na żadne uczucia.

Their bodies were so close together
there was no room for real affection.

Uważaj, by się nie dostać pod
czyjeś koło szczęścia.

Pomyśl, zanim pomyślisz.

Reforma kalendarza nie skróci ciąży.

Analfabeci muszą dyktować.

Dla kogo się kona na krzyżu,
tego nigdy nie ma w pobliżu.

Jeśli kogoś fraszką ugodzę celnie,
to go w pół zabiję, i w pół unieśmiertelnię.

Idealne falsyfikaty muszą dzielić los oryginałów.

Watch out that you do not get crushed under
somebody's wheel of fortune.

Think before you think.

No calendar reform will ever shorten pregnancy.

Illiterates have to dictate.

Those for whom you die on the cross
are never close by.

An apt aphorism half kills,
half immortalizes.

Perfect imitations must share the fate of the originals.

31

Czy nagie kobiety są inteligentne?

Are naked women intelligent?

Żaden pyłek lawiny nie poczuwa się do winy.

Im bliżej do Mekki, tym grzech bardziej lekki.

Każda wiara potrzebuje pręgierza.

Na fukajcie na mężczyzn, panny i mężatki.
Ich cel jest tak przejrzysty jak wasze szatki.

Zwycięstwo w dyskusji należy do perkusji.

Gdy plotki się starzeją, stają się mitami.

Tłum krzyczy jednymi wielkimi ustami,
ale je tysiącem małych.

34

No snowflake in an avalanche ever feels responsible.

The nearer to Mecca the lighter the sins.

Every religion needs its own stakes.

Ladies, do not complain about men;
their aims are as transparent as your clothes.

Percussion wins every discussion.

When gossip gets old it becomes a myth.

The mob shouts with one big mouth
but eats with a thousand little ones.

Sezamie, otwórz się—ja chcę wyjść.

Open Sesame. I want to get out.

Za każdym rogiem czyha kilka
nowych kierunków.

Beyond each corner a number
of new directions lie in wait.

Okno na świat można zasłonić gazetą.

Wieża w Pizie nachyla się pod kątem widzenia turystów.

Jest w nim olbrzymia pustka wypełniona erudycją.

Jaki hormon, taki mormon.

Zło opłaca każde cło.

Wymogi mają kapłani, nie bogi.

Trudno pomału spaść z piedestału.

Nie ufaj swemu sercu, łaknie twej krwi.

The window to the world can be covered by newspaper.

The tower of Piza leans at a tourist angle.

He has a great void filled with erudition.

How much of a mormon—depends on the hormone.

Evil can afford all customs duties.

It's the priests who have demands, not the gods.

It's difficult to fall from a pedestal slowly.

Don't trust the heart, it wants your blood.

Nawet na tronie wycierają się spodnie.

Pants get shiny even on a throne.

Gdy racje są kruche, usztywnia się stanowisko.

Twórzcie o sobie mity,
bogowie nie zaczynali inaczej.

I Mesjasze czekają z niecierpliwością
na swoje przyjście.

"Wracamy zawsze do naszej pierwszej miłości."
Może. Ale w coraz to innych celach.

Fideiści wierzą w zmartwychstanie,
ateiści w "come-back."

Wszystkie drogi prowadzą do Rzymu,
wszystkimi można przejechać mimo.

When reasons are weak, attitudes stiffen.

Create your own myths;
that is how the gods got started.

Messiahs also wait impatiently
for their own coming.

"We always return to our first loves."
Perhaps. But for different reasons.

Believers believe in resurrection,
atheists only in comebacks.

All roads lead to Rome, and you can
by-pass it on all of them.

Kiedy komuś spadną spodnie,
trudno już je podnieść godnie.

When your pants fall down,
it's difficult to pull them up with dignity.

Zwierzęta, nie dowierzajcie ludożercom!

By człowieka torturować,
trzeba znać jego przyjemności.

"Być wolnym jak ptak?"
I gwizdać całe życie jedną, przydzieloną melodię?

Wolność, równość, braterstwo
—jak dojść do czasowników?

Jarzmo ma czasem kształt orderu.

Dwie generacje: myśmy wspólnie śnili,
oni spią z sobą.

Że dopuszczono wówczas do stworzenia świata?

Animals, do not trust cannibals!

To torture a man,
you have to know his pleasures.

"To be free as a bird?"
And to whistle one assigned song all one's life?

Liberty, egality, fraternity
—how do we get to the verbs?

A yoke sometimes has the shape of a medal.

Two generations: we dreamt together,
they sleep together.

How did they ever get a permit to create the world?

Za winy ojców często dopiero
synowie bywają nagrodzeni.

For the sins of their fathers often
only the sons get the rewards.

STANISŁAW JERZY LEC (1909-1966)

W każdym "strachu na wróble"
drzemią ambicje grozy.

ADAM ASNYK (1838-1897)

Tacy poeci, jaka publiczność.

KAZIMIERZ BRANDYS (1916-)

Po czterdziestce mniej oczekuje się od życia,
a więcej od siebie.

JERZY BROSZKIEWICZ (1922-1993)

Geniusz w gruncie rzeczy jest tylko
zaharowanym talentem.

Every scarecrow has a secret
ambition to terrorize.

Like poet, like audience.

After forty, you expect less from life
and more from yourself.

Genius in effect is just
hardworking talent.

Mniejsze zło jest zwykle trwalsze.

W życiu tak się składa, że trzeba chodzić
na pogrzeby tych, których lubimy,
i jubileusze tych, których nie cierpimy.

Należy odpowiadać na drażliwe pytanie,
zanim zostanie zadane.

Czasem można mieć trudności dlatego,
że się je przewiduje.

STANISŁAW BRZOZOWSKI (1876-1911)

Na pogardę zasługuje tylko ten,
kto wie lepiej, a czyni gorzej.

Lesser evil usually lasts longer.

In life one has to go to the funerals
of the ones we like, and to the
anniversaries of those we don't.

Touchy questions should be answered
before they are asked.

Sometimes difficulties come because
you expect them.

STANISŁAW BRZOZOWSKI (1876-1911)

Contemptible is the one
who knows better and acts worse.

55

Od fałszywej skromności lepsza
prawdziwa zarozumiałość.

Wierzyć można tylko w to,
czego nie można wiedzieć.

Łatwiej odbudować zburzone miasto
niż zburzone zaufanie.

Ci, co lękają się śmierci też nie żyją wiecznie.

Im więcej praw, tym więcej przestępców.

Kto raz zgodzi się z niewolą,
nigdy wolny nie będzie.

Honest conceit is better
than false modesty.

You can only believe when
you cannot ascertain.

It is easier to rebuild a destroyed city
than a destroyed trust.

Those who fear death do not live for ever either.

The more laws, the more criminals.

He who accepts slavery once
will never be free.

Z dziesięciu ludzi śpieszących na głos wołającego
"ratunku" dziewięciu podąża tam z ciekawości.

Of ten people responding to a cry of
"help" nine come out of curiosity.

Kobieta oddaje się tylko temu,
którego nie kocha.

JAN CZARNY (1918-1985)

Wszystko co mądre,
powiedział już ktoś inny.

MARIA DĄBROWSKA (1889-1965)

Nie ma romansów nie skonsumowanych.

Jest coś lepszego niż sprawiedliwość
—miłosierdzie.

MICHAŁ CHOROMAŃSKI (1904-1972)

A woman surrenders herself only to
someone she does not love.

JAN CZARNY (1918-1985)

Everything wise has already been said
by someone else.

MARIA DĄBROWSKA (1889-1965)

There are no unconsumated romances.

There is something better than justice
—charity.

Kto cierpieć nie chce, nie będzie panować.

ADOLF DYGASIŃSKI (1839-1902)

Dobrze się zamierzyć znaczy nieraz tyle, co uderzyć.

ZYGMUNT FIJAS (1910-1985)

Wojna dla jednych to via dolorosa,
dla drugich via dollarosa..

ALEKSANDER FREDRO (1793-1876)

Nie każda poprawa na lepsze.

ELŻBIETA DRUŻBACKA (1693-1760)

Who would not suffer, will not rule either.

ADOLF DYGASIŃSKI (1839-1902)

A good faint is as good as a hit.

ZYGMUNT FIJAS (1910-1985)

War; for some a via dolorosa,
for others a via dollarosa.

ALEKSANDER FREDRO (1793-1876)

Not every improvement is for the better.

Przeprosiny—jak wywabiona plama:
zawsze coś zostaje.

Pokazuj po sobie niewiadomość rzeczy,
czym bardziej wiesz wszystko.

Z gniewu w nienawiść droga bardzo bliska.

Nie ma większej radości dla głupiego
jak znaleźć głupszego od siebie.

Żaden jeszcze mężczyzna nie umarł z miłości.

Stary amant jak piec stary:
dużo swędu, mało pary.

An apology—like a cleaned spot;
some of it still remains.

The more you know, the more ignorant
you should appear.

From anger to hate is but a small step.

There is no greater joy for a fool
than to find a greater fool.

No man has yet died of love.

An old lover is like an old stove:
much smoke, little steam.

STEFAN GARCZYŃSKI (ca.1690-1755)

Uśmiech i humor to znak zwycięskiego
górowania nad losem.

POLA GOJAWICZYŃSKA (1896-1963)

Potrzebny jest czyjś śmiech, aby samemu też się
uśmiechnąć.

Smutek to najgorsza poradnia.

WITOLD GOMBROWICZ (1904-1969)

Człowiek nie boi się śmierci lecz cierpienia.

Różnica między intelektualistą zachodnim
a wschodnim na tym polega, iż pierwszy
nie dostał dobrze w d...

STEFAN GARCZYŃSKI (ca.1690-1755)

A smile and good humor are signs
that you dominate your fate.

POLA GOJAWICZYŃSKA (1896-1963)

To smile, you need someone
to smile as well.

Sadness is the worst adviser.

WITOLD GOMBROWICZ (1904-1969)

Man does not fear death, only the suffering.

The difference between western and eastern
intellectuals is that the former have not been
kicked in the ass enough.

To świetny kłamca; ma genialną pamięć.

LUDWIK HIRSZFELD (1884-1954)

Człowiek nauki musi być przygotowany na to, że
w gmachu, który buduje, inni mieszkać będą.

KAROL IRZYKOWSKI (1873-1944)

Kara przychodzi zwykle w ten sposób, że wygląda
jak krzywda. Bóg działa incognito.

Dobrzy chrześcianie wyobrażają sobie, że Pan Bóg
ma najpotężniejszą kartotekę.

A brilliant liar; he has total recall.

Scientists must be prepared that the houses they build will be inhabited by others.

Punishment usually comes disguised as injustice. God acts incognito.

Good Christians imagine that God keeps the best records.

KAROL IRZYKOWSKI (1873-1944)

W polityce zamiast grać, wciąż tasują karty.

EUGENIUSZ IWANICKI (1933-)

Filozofem jest ten, który potrafi milczeć
w różnych językach.

JAROSŁAW IWASZKIEWICZ (1894-1980)

Powiedz mi jakie książki masz w domu,
a powiem ci kim jesteś.

HENRYK JAGODZIŃSKI

Bogaci nudzą się drożej.

70

In politics instead of playing they always shuffle cards.

A philosopher—someone who can be silent
in different languages.

Tell me what books you have at home;
I'll tell you who you are.

The rich are bored more expensively.

Poeci i kanarki zaprzestają śpiewać,
gdy są w parze.

Poets and canaries stop singing
when paired.

Wiara przenosi góry. Ale gdzie?

Gdy cię chwalą poza twoimi plecami,
lepiej się nie oglądaj.

Wszystko jest w ręku Boga. Jedynie Historia
wymknęła się z pod Jego kontroli.

Bóg nie jest graczem,
ale ma słabość do graczy.

STEFAN KISIELEWSKI (1911-1991)

Nieznajomość terminu śmierci umożliwia życie.

Starości nie czujesz—czują ją inni.

Faith moves mountains. But where?

When they praise you behind your back,
don't turn around.

All is in God's hands. Only History managed
to slip out from His control.

God is not a gambler but he does
have a weakness for them.

STEFAN KISIELEWSKI (1911-1991)

Not knowing when you die makes life possible.

You don't feel your old age—others do.

STEFAN KISIELEWSKI (1911-1991)

Naprawdę sławnych żołnierzy ma tylko kraj,
który wygrał wojnę.

FRANCISZEK DIONIZY KNIAŹNIN (1730-1807)

Sen—obraz śmierci.

JAN KOCHANOWSKI (1530-1584)

Prawa są równie jako pajęczyna:
wróbl się przebije, a na muszkę wina.

WESPAZJAN KOCHOWSKI (1633-1700)

Wolność nie miłość, nago nie zwycięża.

Only victorious countries have
truly famous soldiers.

Sleep—preview of death.

The laws are like spiderwebs:
the sparrow flies through, the fly gets the penalty.

Freedom, unlike love, does not win when naked.

Bo słowo w książce—to tylko słowo,
A słowo w uściech—to czyn, mospanie!

Słowami prawdy i kamień przebodzie.

MARIA KONOPNICKA (1842-1910)

Każde szczęście jest progiem nieszczęścia.

JANUSZ KORCZAK (1878-1942)

Nie ma dzieci, są ludzie.

A word in a book is just a word;
a word in the mouth is a deed!

Words of truth will pierce a rock.

MARIA KONOPNICKA (1842-1910)

Every happiness is a threshold to unhappiness.

JANUSZ KORCZAK (1878-1942)

There are no children; just people.

Wszystko niewieścio-piękne silniej nas pociąga niż cała mądrość świata.

Muzyka jest to sztuka smucenia się i cieszenia bez powodu.

Lepiej nie mówić nic, niż mówić o niczym.

Daty są rodzynkami w historii.

Feminine beauty attracts us more than all the wisdom of the world.

TADEUSZ KOTARBIŃSKI (1886-1981)

Music is the ability to be sad or happy without a reason.

Say nothing rather than talk about nothing.

JAN KOTT (1914-)

Dates are the raisins of history.

My rządzimy światem, a nami kobiety.

ZYGMUNT KRASIŃSKI (1812-1859)

Nieszczęście, jak miłość, wiąże ludzi ze sobą.

JÓZEF IGNACY KRASZEWSKI (1812-1887)

Umiesz prawdę mówić? Naucz się też prawdy słuchać.

JAN LAM (1838-1886)

Dopiero zamążpójście pozwala nam utworzyć
dokładne wyobrażenie o kobiecie. Panny
są wszystkie podobne do siebie.

IGNACY KRASICKI (1735-1801)

We rule the world, and are being ruled by women.

ZYGMUNT KRASIŃSKI (1812-1859)

Unhappiness, like love binds people together.

JÓZEF IGNACY KRASZEWSKI (1812-1887)

Can you tell the truth? Learn also to listen to it.

JAN LAM (1838-1886)

Only marriage permits us to form an accurate
image of a woman. Unmarried women
all resemble each other.

83

Kto zmniejszy grzech, ten uszczupla i cnotę.

JERZY LESZCZYŃSKI (1884-1977)

Więcej wśród ludzi krwiopijców niż krwiodawców.

Niejedna para małżeńska jest dowodem, że
nieszczęścia chodzą parami.

Dalej niż krzyk–dochodzi szept.

KORNEL MAKUSZYŃSKI (1884-1953)

Uśmiech to pół pocałunku.

Who belittles sin, diminishes virtue.

There are more bloodsuckers than blood donors.

Quite a few married couples prove that misfortunes come in pairs.

A whisper goes farther than a shout.

A smile is half a kiss.

Piękna kobieta jest jak kaczka—za dużo
na jednego, za mało na dwóch.

A beautiful woman is like a duck—too much
for one, nor enough for two.

Loteria ma przynajmniej jedną zaletę:
przegrywa tylko ten, kto gra.

Kłamstwo ma krótkie nogi,
ale biegnie szybciej od prawdy.

Najgłośniej krzyczy ten, kto przywołuje
do porządku hałasujących.

KRZYSZTOF MĘTRAK (1945-1993)

Wcześnie wykryta inteligencja jest uleczalna.

ADAM MICKIEWICZ (1798-1855)

W słowach tylko chęć widzim, w działaniu potęgę
Trudniej dzień dobrze przeżyć, niż napisać księgę.

ANTONI MARIANOWICZ (1924-)

A lottery has at least one virtue:
you cannot lose if you don't play.

A lie has short legs,
but it runs faster than the truth.

He who calls the noisy ones to
order shouts the loudest.

KRZYSZTOF MĘTRAK (1945-1993)

Intelligence when detected early is curable.

ADAM MICKIEWICZ (1798-1855)

Words convey wishes, while deeds have power; it is
more difficult to live one day well than to write a book.

Ironia—kuzynka bezsiły.

SŁAWOMIR MROŻEK (1930-)

Hasło postkomunizmu:
Ludzie wszystkich planet łączcie się.

Śnieg—woda w proszku.

ADOLF NOWACZYŃSKI (1876-1944)

Pies jest to zwierze domowe, ze wszystkich zwierząt
domowych najmniej znające się na ludziach.

WOJCIECH MŁYNARSKI (1941-)

Irony—cousin of impotency.

SŁAWOMIR MROŻEK (1930-)

A post-communist slogan:
Let people of all planets unite.

Snow—powdered water.

ADOLF NOWACZYŃSKI (1876-1944)

A dog—a domesticated animal
least smart about humans.

Tylko zawiść ma najwięcej rezygnacji w sobie.
Z ochotą nawet zrzekamy się własnych korzyści,
byleśmy zagwarantowaną mieli szkodę bliźniego.

Satyryk to jest głupiec, który na słonia
nastawia łapkę na myszy.

IGNACY PADEREWSKI (1860-1941)

Droga do sukcesu jest pełna kobiet
popychających swych mężów.

WŁODZIMIERZ PERZYŃSKI (1878-1930)

Człowiek się może kochać po całym świecie, ale
żenić się powinien gdzieś niedaleko od domu.

ADOLF NOWACZYŃSKI (1876-1944)

Envy will sacrifice the most.
We readily forgo our own benefits
to assure a neighbor's loss.

A satirist is the fool who sets a mousetrap
to catch an elephant.

IGNACY PADEREWSKI (1860-1941)

The road to success is full of women
pushing their husbands.

WŁODZIMIERZ PERZYŃSKI (1878-1930)

A man can love all over the world, but should
marry somewhere close to home.

Mam tyle rozkoszy w tym, co stworzyłem,
że po prostu nie może być mowy o zasłudze.

BOLESŁAW PRUS (1847-1912)

Litość jest to uczucie równie przykre
dla ofiarującego jak i dla przyjmującego.

Wino robi człowieka przeźroczystym.

JULIAN PRZYBOŚ (1901-1970)

Sztuka pisania jest sztuką skreślania.

I had so much joy in my creations
that there cannot be a question of merit.

BOLESŁAW PRUS (1847-1912)

Pity—a feeling equally disagreeable
for the giver and the recipient.

Wine makes people transparent.

JULIAN PRZYBOŚ (1901-1970)

The art of writing is the art of erasing.

Bo ci najlepszy zysk mają,
co się w nich ludzie kochają.

WŁADYSŁAW STANISŁAW REYMONT (1867-1925)

Życie nie daje nam tego, co chcemy,
ale to, co ma dla nas.

TADEUSZ RITTNER (1873-1921)

Nic tak nie łagodzi rany psychicznej
jak zapach kolejowego dymu.

Są ludzie podobni do ślepca,
co ukradł i zjadł własną kurę!

Those fare best who
are loved by people.

Life does not grant us what we wish,
but what it has for us.

Nothing soothes a psychic wound better
than the smell of a train's smoke.

Some people are like the blind man
who stole and ate his own chicken!

Śmiać się prawdziwie umieją tylko ludzie poważni.

MAGDALENA SAMOZWANIEC (1899-1972)

Jesteśmy dobrzy dla drugich,
aby się sobie więcej podobać.

Śmiech i kpiny—to niejednokrotnie płacz mędrca.

Starość posiada te same apetyty co młodość
tylko nie te same zęby.

Niedyskrecją męską wybrukowane jest piekło.

Słowa są nieraz plotkami naszych myśli.

Only serious people can truly laugh.

MAGDALENA SAMOZWANIEC (1899-1972)

We are good to others
to like ourselves more.

Laughter and jokes—often a wise man's cry.

Old age and youth have the same appetites
but not the same teeth.

Hell is paved with male indiscretions.

Words are often the gossips of our thoughts.

Ciekawość—pierwszy stopień do zdrady.

Curiosity—the first step to betrayal.

Każdy mężczyzna uważa siebie za znakomitego
aktora, który powinien mieć szersze audytorium
—jedna kobieta mu nie wystarcza.

Every man thinks himself a great actor
who deserves a wider audience
—one woman is not enough.

Przyjaźń po wygaśnięciu miłości
jest jak dym po pożarze.

HENRYK SIENKIEWICZ (1846-1916)

Im pisarz znakomitszy,
tym mniej pisze po literacku.

Jakie społeczeństwo, taka literatura.

Tylko to co przyszło z trudem,
czyta się łatwo.

Przyjaźń z kobietą
zawsze kończy się miłością.

Friendship after love
is like smoke after a fire.

The more superb a writer,
the less literary is his writing.

Like society, like literature.

Only that which comes with great effort
is easy to read.

Friendship with a woman
always ends in love.

W teatrze bywa się
głównie dla antraktów.

Kościół twój tam, skąd boskie płynie ci natchnienie,
A nie tam, gdzie krzyż widzisz, belki i kamienie.

Na twoim czole z przerażeniem czytam
Ostatni stopień wszystkich nieszczęść—nudę.

Tango—to smutna myśl, którą się tańczy.

One goes to the theater
mainly for the intermissions.

Your church is where you feel God's inspiration;
not where you see the cross, walls and stones.

On your face I sadly note
the last stage of all misfortunes—boredom.

Tango—A sad thought to which one can dance.

Śmierci tak potrzeba uczyć się jak życia.

HUGO DIONIZY STEINHAUS (1887-1972)

Miłość robi odkrycia, rozpusta wynalazki.

ANDRZEJ STRUG (1873-1937)

Nigdy—głupie słowo...
tego przecie człowiek nigdy nie ogarnie.

ALEKSANDER ŚWIĘTOCHOWSKI (1849-1938)

Więcej mądrości nauczy cię
jedna żona niż tysiąc kochanek.

One needs to learn death as we learn life.

Love makes discoveries, dissipation makes inventions.

Never—a silly word.
One can never comprehend it.

You will learn more wisdom from
one wife than from a thousand mistresses.

Złodziej łatwo porozumiałby się z policjantem,
gdyby mu nie przeszkadzał okradziony.

MIECZYSŁAW MICHAŁ SZARGAN

Wiara przenosi góry. Na plecach wiernych.

JAN SZTAUDYNGER (1904-1970)

Dawniej udawałem cnotę, dziś udaję ochotę.

Z grama korzyści, kilo zawiści.

Prawdziwych przyjaciół poznaje się w biedzie
Ale lepiej się łudzić przy dobrym obiedzie.

A thief could easily come to terms with a policeman
if it was not for the victim.

Faith moves mountains. On the backs of the faithful.

Once I faked virtue, now I fake desire.

An ounce of gain, a pound of envy.

A friend in need is a friend indeed...
but it's better to feed illusions at a good dinner.

Nigdy mi nie odmówiły te które mi się śniły.

The women I dreamt of never refused me.

Bóg tyle cudnych dziewek stwarza,
a potem wszyscy huzia na dziwkarza.

Doświadczenie—ten dar nieba masz
gdy ci go już nie trzeba.

WACŁAW SZYMANOWSKI (1821-1886)

Kto się kochał sto razy, ten nie zna miłości.

SZYMON SZYMONOWIC (1558-1629)

Wielki swar trzeba gasić szkodami małymi.

Mężniejszy są, co sławy,
 nie chłosty się boją.

114

God makes so many beautiful women...
but they always scold a womanizer.

Experience—God's gift
when you no longer need it.

WACŁAW SZYMANOWSKI (1821-1886)

Who has loved a hundred times, does not know love.

SZYMON SZYMONOWIC (1558-1629)

Big quarrels should be settled with little losses.

More courageous is he
who fears not the whip but fame.

KAZIMIERZ PRZERWA TETMAJER (1865-1940)

Kiedy tysiąc baranów pozna, że razem mają 2,000
rogów, nie ma tam co robić ani pasterz, ani pies.

WIESŁAW TRZASKALSKI

Pustą głową łatwiej jest potakiwać.

JULIAN TUWIM (1894-1953)

Nie pożądaj żony bliźniego swego nadaremno.

Tragedia—zakochać się w twarzy,
a ożenić się z całą dziewczyną.

Rzuć szczęściarza do wody,
a wypłynie z rybą w zębach.

116

When 1,000 sheep realize that they have 2,000
horns... watch out shepherd and sheepdog!

WIESŁAW TRZASKALSKI

An empty head nods more easily.

JULIAN TUWIM (1894-1953)

Do not desire your neighbor's wife in vain.

Tragedy—to fall in love with a face,
and marry the whole woman.

Throw a lucky man into water
and he'll surface with a fish in his mouth.

Życie—dożywotna kara śmierci.

Pesymista twierdzi, że wszystkie kobiety to nierządnice.
Optymista nie jest tego zdania, ale ma nadzieję.

Wierność—silne swędzenie
z zakazem podrapania się.

Nawet najpiękniejsze nogi gdzieś się kończą.

Różnica między wielbłądem a człowiekiem:
wielbłąd może pracować nie pijąc przez cały tydzień;
człowiek może przez tydzień pić nie pracując.

Koń ma cztery nogi. Po jednej na każdym rogu.

Life—a lifelong death sentence.

A pessimist says all women are loose.
An optimist does not, but he has hopes.

Fidelity—a strong itch
with a prohibition to scratch.

Even the most beautiful legs end somewhere.

The difference between camels and men;
a camel can work a week and not drink;
a man can drink a week and not work.

A horse has four legs. One at each corner.

JULIAN TUWIM (1894-1953)

Choroba—medalomania.

A new sickness—medalomania.

120

Sumienie jest to ten cichy głosik,
który szepcze, że ktoś patrzy.

Egoista—ten, który dba więcej o siebie niż o mnie.

Cnotliwa dziewczyna nigdy nie lata za chłopcem.
Czy kto widział, żeby pułapka goniła mysz?

Sukces—coś, czego przyjaciele nigdy ci nie wybaczą.

Rodzynka—stroskane winogrono.

Pchła—owad co zszedł na psy.

Corpus delicti—rozkoszne ciało.

Conscience; that quiet voice
which whispers that someone is watching.

Egoist is someone who cares more for himself than me.

A virtuous girl never chases after boys;
who ever saw a mousetrap chasing mice?

Success—something your friends will never forgive you.

Raisin—a worried grape.

A flea—an insect which has gone to the dogs.

Corpus delicti—a delicious body.

In partibus infidelium—zdradza mnie,
ale częściowo.

Dowcip jest to bardzo ważny artykuł
w toalecie kobiet.

Nie można być dość wybrednym
w wyborze rodziców.

Nic tak nie wzrusza mężczyzny jak łzy kobiety,
którą kochać zaczyna, i nic nie drażni go tak,
jak łzy kobiety, którą kochać przestaje.

In partibus infidelium—she is unfaithful
but only partly.

Wit is a very important part
of a woman's outfit.

You can never be too picky
when choosing parents.

Nothing moves a man as much as the tears of the
woman he begins to love, and nothing irritates him
as much as the tears of the woman he loves no longer.

JAN ZACHARIASIEWICZ (1825-1906)

Miłość jest to śliczne, złote pudełeczko, w którym
schowany leży starannie zrobiony rachuneczek.

JERZY ZAWIEJSKI (1902-1969)

Wszystko, co najważniejsze,
staje się tylko raz w życiu.

Love is a dainty golden little box, in which you will find a carefully prepared and concealed little bill.

JERZY ZAWIEJSKI (1902-1969)

The most important things in life
happen only once.

Polish Proverbs

To complete this tour of Polish wit and wisdom here are some proverbs which are either original—a rare occurrence in the world of proverbs—or express a universal idea in an unusual fashion worth remembering.

Thus a universal proverb "Man proposes, God disposes," in Polish corresponds to: "Chłop strzela, Pan Bóg kule nosi" or literally: "Man shoots and God carries the bullets."

The proverbs had been translated by Helen Stankiewicz Zand (*Polish Proverbs*, 1961) and are reproduced here by kind permission of The Polish American Journal, the publisher of Mrs. Zand's book.

Czym skorupka za młodu nasiąknie,
tym na starość trąci.

Nie ma dalekiej drogi do mojej niebogi.

Miłość bez pieniędzy, wrota do nędzy.

Dobra żona, mężowa korona.

Gdzie ogon rządzi, głowa błądzi.

Gdzie diabeł nie zdoła, babę pośle.

Głos matki, głos Boga.

What the shell absorbs in youth,
of that it will smell in old age.

The way is never long to one's beloved.

Love without money, gateway to misery.

A good wife is the husband's crown.

Where the tail rules, the head blunders.

Where the devil can't manage, he'll send a woman.

Mother' s voice is God's voice.

Nie ta matka co urodzi,
lecz ta co wychowa.

Gość w dom, Bóg w dom.

Co po trzeźwemu myśli, to po pijanemu powie.

Dobrego karczma nie zepsuje,
a złego kościół nie naprawi.

Jak Kuba Bogu, tak Bóg Kubie.

Kto pod kim dołki kopie, sam w nie wpada.

Jeszcze się nie urodził,
coby wszystkim dogodził.

She is not the mother who bears,
but the one who rears.

A guest in the house is God in the house.

What one thinks when sober, one says when drunk.

The tavern will not spoil a good man,
nor the church mend a bad one.

As Jacob to God, so God to Jacob.

Who digs pits under others falls into them himself.

The man has not yet been born
who can please everyone.

Nie strzelaj prochem kiedy można grochem.

Strzeżonego Pan Bóg strzeże.

Tonący brzytwy się chwyta.

Lepszy łut szczęścia niż funt złota.

Nie każdemu skrzypce grają.

Pieniądz dobry sługa lecz zły przewodnik.

Za wysokie progi na moje nogi.

Pies szczeka, kareta jedzie.

Do not shoot with powder when you can shoot peas.

God guards the guarded.

The drowning man clutches at a razor.

Better an ounce of luck than a pound of gold.

The violin does not play for everyone.

Money is a good servant but a poor guide.

The threshold's too high for my feet.

Dog barks, carriage rides on.

Zastaw się, a postaw się.

Kto chce psa uderzyć, kija znajdzie.

Pańskie oko konia tuczy.

Zamierzać się motyką na słońce.

Mądrej głowie dość dwie słowie.

Słowo wylata wróblem, a powraca wołem.

Go into debt but make a good showing.

Who wants to hit a dog will find a stick.

The master's eye fattens the horse.

Shake a hoe at the sun.

To a wise head two words are sufficient.

The word flies out a sparrow, but comes back an ox.

Also from Hippocrene Books . . .

A Polish Heritage Publication
The Polish Heritage Art Calendar
Published since 1986, this monthly wall calendar (12" x 24" when open)
contains 12 reproductions of the best of Polish paintings from museums and
private collections all over the world, including the Polish museums in
Chicago, Warsaw, Cracow, Lwow, Poznan, Wroclaw, as well as Rapperswil.
   "The paintings selected are the best in Polish art, and the high quality of
the reproductions makes the calendar itself a work of art."
                    —*Nowy Dziennik*
   "The reproductions alone are worth the price of the calendar."
                    —*Polish American Journal*
13 color illustrations   0-7818-0551-1 $10.95   (640)

A Polish Heritage Publication
American Phrasebook for Poles, 2nd Edition
by Jacek Galazka & Janusz Bibik
"This book is excellent—well thought out and executed, it is enormously
useful. There is nothing like it."
                    —Professor Stanislaw Baranczak, Harvard University
153 pages   5½ x 8½   0-7818-0554-6 $8.95pb   (644)

A Polish Heritage Publication
The Polish Heritage Songbook
"The collection comprises the music and Polish lyrics for 74 of the most
popular folk and military songs sung by the legionnaires in World War I, as
well as songs the scouts sing. Each song is accompanied by a splendid
drawing by Szymon Kobylinski and an English language commentary on the
songs' origins is provided by Stanislaw Werner.... The Polish Heritage
Songbook is a useful compilation and will be much in demand when friends
meet and want to sing but do not remember all the words."
                    —Jerzy R. Krzyzanowski, *Przeglad Polski*
65 illustrations, 80 songs
166 pages   6 x 9   0-7818-0425-6 $14.95pb   (496)

A Polish Heritage Publication
Song, Dance & Customs of Peasant Poland
by Sula Benet with preface from Margaret Mead
"This charming fable-like book is one long remembrance of rural, peasant Poland which almost does not exist anymore... but is worthwhile to safeguard the memory of what once was... because what [Benet] writes is a piece of all of us, now in the past but very much a part of our cultural background." —*Przeglad Polski*
illustrations
247 pages   5½ x 8½   0-7818-0447-7 $24.95hc   (209)

Polish Herbs, Flowers & Folk Medicine
by Sophie Hodorowicz Knab
Besides taking the reader on a guided tour through monastery, castle and cottage gardens, this book provides details on over one hundred herbs and flowers and how they were used in folk medicine as well as in everyday life, traditions, and customs.
illustrations, woodcuts
207 pages   5½ x 8½   0-7818-0319-5 $19.95hc   (573)

Polish Customs, Traditons & Foklore, Revised Edition
by Sophie Hodorowicz Knab with an introduction by Rev. Czeslaw Krysa
Now in its fourth printing!
This unique reference is arranged by month, showing the various occasions, feasts and holidays prominent in Polish culture—beginning with December it continues through Holy Week customs, superstitions, beliefs and rituals associated with farming, Pentecost, Corpus Christi, midsummer, harvest festivals, wedding rites, namedays, birth and death. Line illustrations complete this rich and varied treasury of folklore. Now updated with a new chapter on "Customs for Kids"!
340 pages   5½ x 8½   0-7818-0515-5 $19.95hc   (500)

Polish Weddings: Customs & Traditions

A unique planning guide for Americans who want to organize and celebrate a Polish-style wedding. Sections titled Engagement, Bridal Flowers, Wedding Cothes, ceremony, reception and even Baby Names, will assist the bride- and groom-to-be through every step of the wedding process. Special tips on "How to Draw from the Past" at the end of each chapter provide helpful suggestions on how to incorporate Polish tradition into the modern wedding, to make it a truly distinctive and unforgettable event.

250 pages   5½ x 8½   0-7818-0530-9 $19.95hc   (641)

Polish Folk Dances & Songs: A Step-by-Step Guide
by Ada Dziewanowska

The most comprehensive and definitive book on Polish dance in the English language, with in-depth descriptions of over 80 of Poland's most characteristic and interesting dances. The author provides step-by-step instruction on position, basic steps and patterns for each dance. Includes over 400 illustrations depicting steps and movements and over 90 appropriate musical selections. Ada Dziewanowska is the artistic director and choreographer of the Syrena Polish Folk Dance Ensemble of Milwaukee, Wisconsin.

800 pages   6 x 9   0-7818-0420-5 $39.50hc   (508)

Polish Heritage Cookery
by Robert and Maria Strybel

New illustrated edition of a bestseller with 20 color photographs! Over 2,200 recipes in 29 categories, written especially for Americans!

"An encyclopedia of Polish cookery and a wonderful thing to have."
   —Julia Child, *Good Morning America*
   "*Polish Heritage Cookery* is the best [Polish] cookbook printed on the English market!"   —*Polish American Cultural Network*
16 pages color photographs
915 pages   6 x 9   0-7818-0558-9 $39.95hc   (658)

Polish Fables, Bilingual Edition

by Ignacy Krasicki and translated by Gerard T. Kapolka

Sixty-five fables by eminent Polish poet Bishop Ignacy Krasicki are translated into English by Gerard Kapolka. With great artistry, the author used contemporary events and human relations to show a course to guide human conduct. For over two centuries, Krasicki's fables have entertained and instructed his delighted readers. This bilingual gift edition contains twenty illustrations by Barbara Swidzinska, a well known Polish artist. Illustrations

250 pages   6 x 9   0-7818-0548-1 $19.95hc   (646)

Glass Mountain: Twenty-Eight Ancient Polish Folktales and Fables

Retold by W.S. Kuniczak and illustrated by Pat Bargielski

"It is an heirloom book to pass on to children and grandchildren. A timeless book, with delightful illustrations, it will make a handsome additon to any library and will be a most treasured gift."

     —*Polish American Cultural Network*

160 pages   7 x 10   0-7818-0552-X $16.95hc   (645)

Treasury of Polish Love Poems, Quotations & Proverbs

Miroslaw Lipinski, editor and translator

Works by Krasinski, Sienkiewicz and Mickiewicz are included among 100 selections by 44 authors

128 pages   0-7818-0297-0 $11.95   (185)

Audiobook: 0-7818-0361-6 $12.95   (576)

Treasury of Classic Polish Love Short Stories
in Polish and English
Edited by Miroslaw Lipinski
This charming gift volume delves into Poland's rich literary tradition to bring you classic love stories from five renowned authors. It explores love's many romantic, joyous, as well as melancholic facets, and is destined to inspire love and keep its flame burning bright.
128 pages   0-7818-0513-91 $11.95   (603)

Dictionary of 1,000 Polish Proverbs
Edited by Miroslaw Lipinski
Proverbs are arranged side-by-side with their English equivalents and are organized alphabetically by key word. An index organizes the proverbs by English subject.
141 pages   5 x 7   0-7818-0482-5 $11.95pb   (568)

(All prices subject to change.)

TO PURCHASE HIPPOCRENE BOOKS contact your local bookstore, or write to: HIPPOCRENE BOOKS, 171 Madison Avenue, New York, NY 10016. Please enclose check or money order, adding $5.00 shipping (UPS) for the first book and $.50 for each additional book.